# CELEBRATE WONDER

### Includes One Room Sunday School®

**Vol. 4 • No. 4 • Summer 2024**

#### EDITORIAL / DESIGN TEAM

Megan Teegarden. . . . . . . . . . . . . . . .Editor

Selena Cunningham. . . . . . . . . . . . . .Editor

Pamela Crosby . . . . . . . . . Production Editor

Matt Allison . . . . . Production & Design Manager

#### ADMINISTRATIVE TEAM

Rev. Brian K. Milford. . . . .President and Publisher

Marjorie M. Pon . Associate Publisher and Editor of Church School Publications

Cover design by *Celebrate Wonder* Design Team. Cover photos: Shutterstock; cover illustrations: Brave Union.

Art Credits: pp. 10, 11, 13, 15, 17, 19, 25: Shutterstock; pp. 5, 23, 29: Tatevik Avakyan/ Illustration Online LLC; pp. 3, 20: Carolyn Williams/ Gwen Walters; p. 7: Becky Fawson/Gwen Walters; pp. 4, 9: Robbie Short; p. 21: Mary Grace Corpus/ Gwen Walters; p. 27: Adobe Stock; Background art unless otherwise noted: Shutterstock

Celebrate Wonder All Ages, Take-Home Activity Sheets: An official resource for The United Methodist Church approved by Discipleship Ministries and published quarterly by Abingdon Press, a division of The United Methodist Publishing House, 810 12th Avenue South, Nashville TN 37203. Copyright © 2023 Abingdon Press. All rights reserved.. Printed in the United States of America.

To order copies of this publication, call toll free: **800-672-1789.** You may fax your order to 800-445-8189. Telecommunication Device for the Deaf/ Telex Telephone: 800-227-4091. Or order online at **cokesbury.com**. Use your Cokesbury account, Visa, Discover, or Mastercard.

For information concerning permission to reproduce any material in this publication, write to Rights and Permissions, The United Methodist Publishing House, 810 12th Avenue South, Nashville TN 37203.

You may also fax your request to 615-749-6128 or email *permissions@umpublishing.org.*

COMMON ENGLISH BIBLE Scripture quotations are taken from the Common English Bible, copyright 2011. Used by permission. All rights reserved.

# CONTENTS

# SCOPE AND SEQUENCE
## FALL 2023–SUMMER 2024

| Fall 2023 | Winter 2023–24 | Spring 2024 | Summer 2024 |
|---|---|---|---|
| **UNIT 1: CREATIVITY** | **UNIT 1: JOY** | **UNIT 1: REMEMBER** | **UNIT 1: PEACE** |
| God Creates the Earth<br>Genesis 1:1-19 | Mary's Joy<br>Luke 1:26-38, 46-56 | Jesus Washes Feet<br>John 13:1-17 | Abraham and Lot<br>Genesis 13:1-18 |
| God Creates Living Things<br>Genesis 1:20-25 | Joseph's Joy<br>Matthew 1:18-24 | The Last Supper<br>Luke 22:14-20 | David and Abigail<br>1 Samuel 25:1-42 |
| God Creates People<br>Genesis 1:26–2:4 | Jesus Brings Joy<br>Luke 2:1-7 | Praying in the Garden<br>Luke 22:39-46 | Be Peaceful<br>Psalm 23:1-6 |
| God Creates Helpers<br>Genesis 2:10-23 | Joyous News<br>Luke 2:8-20 | Jesus Enters Jerusalem<br>Matthew 21:1-11 | Esther<br>Book of Esther |
| | The Magi<br>Matthew 2:1-12 | Resurrection<br>Matthew 28:1-10 | Peacemakers<br>Matthew 5:1-12 |
| **UNIT 2: FAITH** | **UNIT 2: INCLUDE** | **UNIT 2: SHARE** | **UNIT 2: BELONG** |
| Abraham and Sarah<br>Genesis 12:1-9 | Jesus' Baptism<br>Matthew 3:13-17 | The Great Commission<br>Matthew 28:16-20 | Babel<br>Genesis 11:1-9 |
| God's Promise to Abraham<br>Genesis 15:1-6 | Calling the Disciples<br>Matthew 4:18-22 | Peter and John<br>Acts 3:1-10 | Mephibosheth<br>2 Samuel 9:1-13 |
| Abraham's Visitors<br>Genesis 18:1-14 | Showing Love<br>Matthew 5:43-48 | Believers Share<br>Acts 4:32-3 | The Woman at the Well<br>John 4:4-30, 39-42 |
| Isaac Is Born<br>Genesis 21:1-7 | God's Kingdom<br>Luke 13:18-21 | Choosing the Seven<br>Acts 6:1-7 | Peter's Dream<br>Acts 10:1-48 |
| Jacob and Esau<br>Genesis 25:19-28 | | | |
| **UNIT 3: BLESSING** | **UNIT 3: GUIDE** | **UNIT 3: LOVE** | **UNIT 3: COURAGE** |
| The Birthright<br>Genesis 25:29-34 | The Lord's Prayer<br>Matthew 6:5-15 | Peter and Tabitha<br>Acts 9:36-43 | Rahab<br>Joshua 2:1-24 |
| The Blessing<br>Genesis 27:1-45 | Jesus Calms the Storm<br>Mark 4:35-41 | The Church Grows<br>Acts 9:26-31 | Ruth and Naomi<br>Book of Ruth |
| Jacob's Ladder<br>Genesis 28:10-22 | Mary and Martha<br>Luke 10:38-42 | Pentecost<br>Acts 2:1-12 | Mary Anoints Jesus<br>John 12:1-8 |
| A Peaceable Kingdom<br>Isaiah 11:6-9 | Zacchaeus<br>Luke 19:1-10 | Love in Action<br>Romans 12:9-18 | Lydia<br>Acts 16:11-15 |

# Abraham and Lot

Making Peace

1. Cut out the four circles.
2. Sandwich a straw or pencil between the circle of Abraham with two sheep and the circle of land with a tree in the middle, pictures facing outward.
3. Glue or tape the circles together, keeping the straw or pencil in between.
4. Do the same for the circle of Lot with two sheep and the circle of land with all green grass.
5. Twirl each spinner between your hands to show which land Abraham and Lot settled on.

# David and Abigail
Finger Puppets

1. Cut out the three finger puppets and tape or glue the tabs together.
2. Use the puppets to tell the story.

# Be Peaceful
Sheep Ears

1. Cut out the sheep ears and glue on cotton balls.
2. Punch a hole on each side, and tie a piece of yarn through each hole.
3. Tie the lengths of yarn together at the back of the head.

# Esther
Queen Esther

1. Cut out Esther, her crown, and the throne.
2. Glue the pieces on a separate piece of paper and complete the picture.
3. Use your picture to help tell the Bible story.

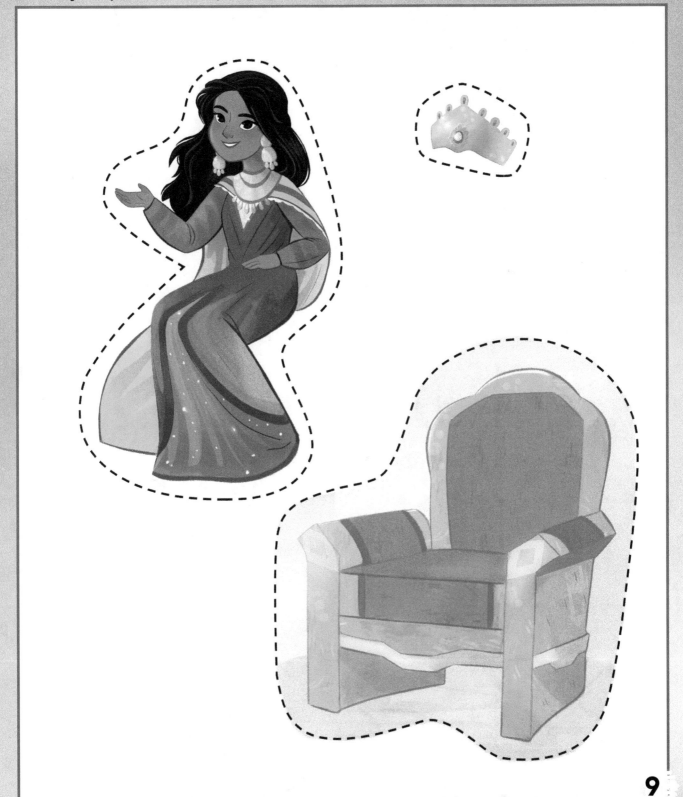

# Peacemakers
Blessed Are Peacemakers

Circle all the ways to make peace.

Walk away.

Use your words.

Ask for help.

Relax.

Look at the situation differently.

# Peacemakers
Bee-Attitudes

**Match each bee with the correct face. How are you feeling today?**

Kind

Peaceful

Happy

Sad

Worried

# Babel
## Storytelling Cards

Cut out the cards. Put the cards in order to help you retell the Bible story.

# Mephibosheth
"You Belong" Place Mat

Color and decorate the place mat. Cut out the place mat and glue to a piece of construction paper, and/or cover the place mat in contact paper.

# The Woman at the Well
Clay Jar

1. Color the jar and cut out the jar.
2. Glue long strips of blue yarn coming out of the top of the clay jar, overflowing onto the side like water.

# Peter's Dream
Storytelling Pieces

1. Cut out the storytelling pieces.
2. Glue the pieces on a separate piece of construction paper and draw your own details. Use your picture to help you retell the Bible story.

# Rahab
Eye Spies

Circle Rahab and the two spies in the city scene.

# Rahab
Rope Maze

Help the two men get to Rahab's house.

# Ruth and Naomi
Strong Women

Who is a woman that you know who is strong and courageous? Write her a letter or draw her a picture, and share what you admire about her. Cut out your letter and place it in an envelop to deliver.

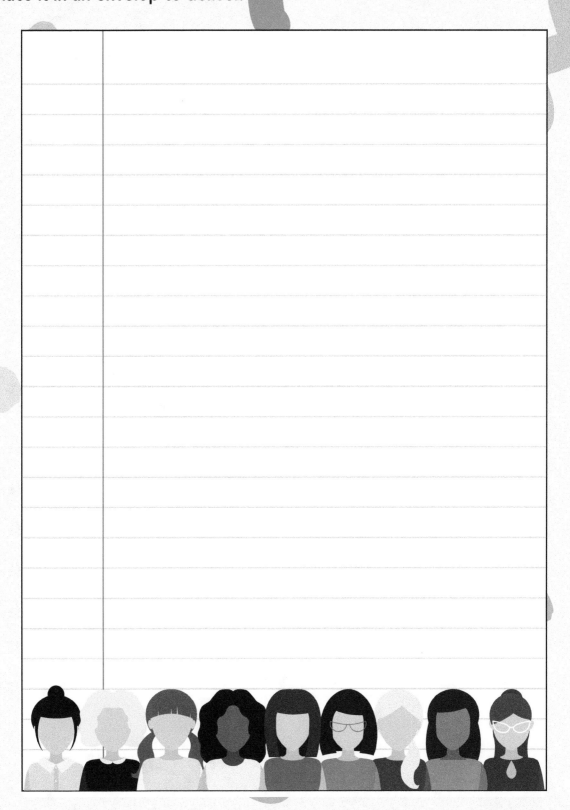

# Mary Anoints Jesus
## Ways to Serve Jesus

In our Bible story, Mary used her hands and hair to serve Jesus. Finish the sentences with ways you can use your body to serve Jesus. Cut out the cards and keep them as a reminder to serve Jesus.

I can use my brain to serve by...

I can use my ears to serve by...

I can use my feet to serve by...

I can use my eyes to serve by...

I can use my voice to serve by...

I can use my hands to serve by...

# Lydia
## My Church

Cut out the church on the outer solid lines.
Fold on the dotted lines, and glue the tabs in place.

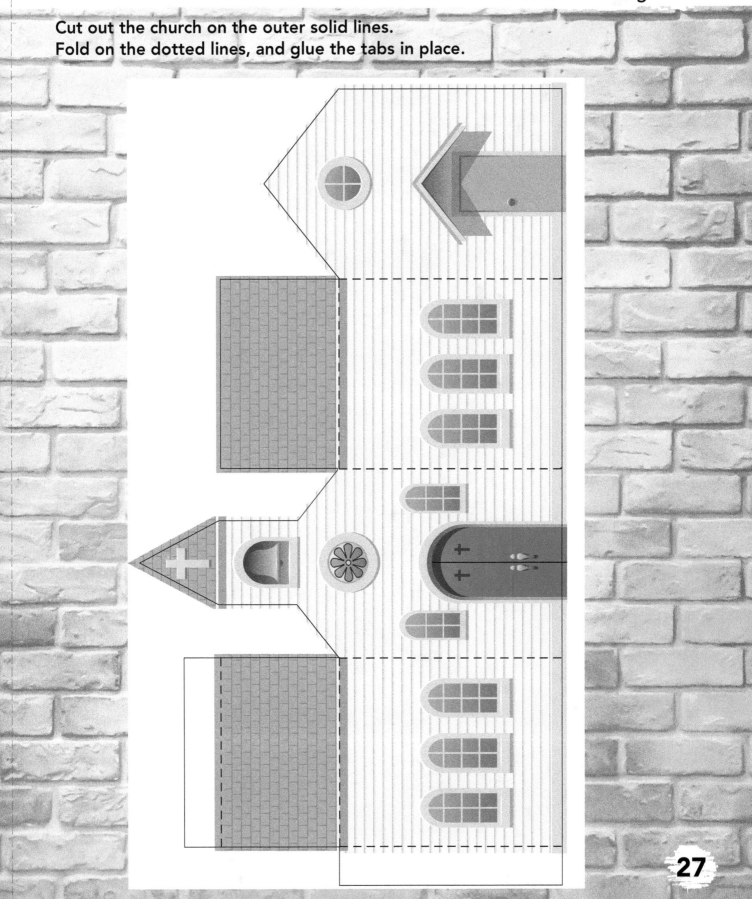

# Jesus Teaches Peace
Bonus Coloring Page

Jesus teaches us many things! Think about what Jesus means to you as you color the page.

# Answers/Extra Page

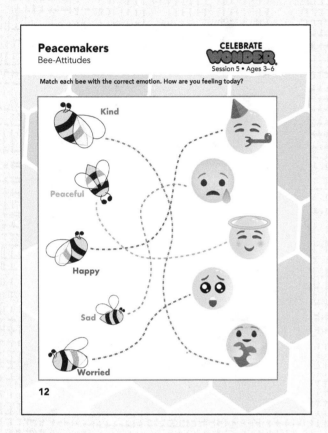

Printed in the USA
CPSIA information can be obtained
at www.ICGtesting.com
LVHW082352160224
772019LV00001B/1